Word Bird's

New Friend

Published in the United States of America by The Child's World®, Inc.
PO Box 326
Chanhassen, MN 55317-0326
800-599-READ
www.childsworld.com

Project Manager Mary Berendes
Editor Katherine Stevenson, Ph.D.
Designer Ian Butterworth

Library of Congress Cataloging-in-Publication Data
Moncure, Jane Belk.
Word Bird's new friend / by Jane Belk Moncure.
p. cm.
Summary: When a new student arrives at school,
Word Bird does his best to help her feel at home.
ISBN 1-56766-844-5 (lib. : alk. paper)
[1. First day of school—Fiction. 2. Schools—Fiction.
3. Friendship—Fiction. 4. Birds—Fiction. 5. Kangaroos—Fiction.]
I. Title.
PZ7.M739 Woj 2002
[E]—dc21
2001006053

Word Bird's

New Friend

by Jane Belk Moncure

illustrated by Chris McEwan

One morning Miss Beary said,
"We have someone new in our class.
This is Little Kangaroo."
"Hi, Little Kangaroo," everyone said.

Little Kangaroo did not say a word.
Little Kangaroo was too shy and afraid.
"Come with me. I will show you around,"
said Word Bird.

Word Bird and Little Kangaroo
watched Frog work a counting puzzle.
"I cannot do that," said Little Kangaroo.

Little Kangaroo and Word Bird
watched Cat make words.
"I cannot do that," said Little Kangaroo.

Hen and Duck were playing store.
"You can play, too," they said.
But Little Kangaroo said, "No."

Dog was making a dinosaur out of clay. "You can make one, too," Dog said to Little Kangaroo. But Little Kangaroo did not want to play with clay.

Little Kangaroo did not want to cut
with scissors or make things with
paste. Little Kangaroo did not want
to do anything.

"Let's go and watch Bee," said
Word Bird.

Bee was painting a picture of a boat.
"Hi, Little Kangaroo," said Bee.
"Hi," said Little Kangaroo. "I like boats."

"Good," said Word Bird. "I know what we can do. We can build a boat."
"Yes," said Little Kangaroo. "Let's do that."

They went right to work, making
a boat with blocks. Little Kangaroo
began to smile.

Word Bird found two hats in the
dress-up box.
"We can be boat captains," Word Bird said.
"Let's sail around the world."

After a while, Miss Beary came by.
"My, what a fine boat," she said.
"Should we have story time here today?"
"Yes," said Little Kangaroo.

Everyone jumped in. Miss Beary read
a story about boats.

She read it two times.
The captains smiled.

"It's time for music," said Miss Beary.
Word Bird and Little Kangaroo were
partners. They sat on the floor and
made a boat with their feet.

They went back and forth as they
sang, "Row, row, row your boat,"
over and over.

At lunchtime, Word Bird gave
Little Kangaroo a cookie.
"Thank you," said Little Kangaroo.

At recess, Word Bird and Little
Kangaroo went up and down on
the seesaw until Miss Beary called.

"It's time for a potato-sack race," said Miss Beary. Everyone came running.

Word Bird was captain of one team.
Frog was captain of the other.
"Hop around your pole and back again,"
said Miss Beary.

Away they hopped, around their poles
and back again.

"Hop fast! Hop fast!" everyone yelled.

Finally, Dog and Little Kangaroo
started out. Little Kangaroo went
hop, hop, hop very fast.

But just after hopping around the pole,
Little Kangaroo tripped and fell.
Dog hopped right on by.

Word Bird helped Little Kangaroo up.
But it was too late.

Frog's team won the race.
"It's okay," said Word Bird to
Little Kangaroo.
"You hop fast. The next time we will win."

Soon it was time to go home.
"I'll see you tomorrow," said Word Bird.
"You bet!" said Little Kangaroo.

"What did you do at school today?"
Papa asked that night. Word Bird
thought for a minute.
"I lost a potato-sack race, but I won
a friend," Word Bird said.

Can you read Word Bird's
win-a-friend words?

Be kind.

Be helpful.

Be friendly.

Smile.

You can win
friends, too!